50 Instant Pot Bake:

Quick and Easy Recipes Fc

Table of contents

What is an instant pot?

If you are not yet familiar with the term, you might be wondering what an instant pot is and what all the fuss is all about.

An instant pot is a versatile multi-cooker that can serve as a slow cooker or a pressure cooker. It can also sauté and steam, and can be used for baking or yogurt making. What an instant pot primarily does is to cook your food at the most suitable temperature and pressure, giving you the best result and removing all the guesswork.

The instant pot is the go-to cooking essential when you need a quickly prepared dish or if you are short on cooking time. It also comes in handy if you generally need a pot that can cook a variety of dishes all in one depending on your preference. Yes! From veggies to meat sautéing, down to cooking a whole chicken, hard-boiled eggs, and even baking, this piece of magical kitchen appliance does it all. For this book, however, we'll focus on the instant pot bakery aspect.

What can you bake in an instant pot?

With the innovative nature of the instant pot, there seem to be no limits to what you can achieve when it comes to cooking, and baking isn't left out either. You will be surprised at the wide variety of delicacies you will be able to churn out with this one-stop-shop for cooking convenience. From over two hundred different types of cakes to baked beans, potatoes, brownies, and oatmeal, your instant pot can genuinely become your multi-purpose makeshift oven. Bread is not left out, and the exciting news is that all instant pot bakes turn out fine and arguably as delicious as your traditional oven bakes.

There have even been testimonies of instant pot cheesecakes being less dense than the traditional oven variety, added to the reduced cooking time (30 minutes against nearly an hour in the oven). Baking is one use of the instant pot that you should really explore.

Safety measures while using the instant pot

Even though this book is focusing on how to bake with your instant pot, it is worthwhile to take note of some general safety measures while using the instant pot. These measures should be adhered to, to ensure safety and prolong the lifespan of your multi-purpose kitchen accessory. They are as follows;

1. Do not leave your house or forget the instant pot when it is in use and going up in pressure. Most people run the risk of forgetting that the instant pot is in use. They get distracted or carried away because the instant pot is an electronic device with timers and all, and no steam comes out from anywhere to indicate usage. However, you should monitor your instant pot at all times whenever it is in use.

2. Do not pressure-fry with your instant pot or any other pressure cooker for that matter.

3. Keep in mind that the instant pot mostly needs a minimum of 1 cup of liquid to get to, and maintain pressure. This myth is, however, debatable and will depend on your instant pot model. Also, avoid using hard alcohols as much as possible.

4. Do not overfill your instant pot; else it will boil over and leave you at the danger of having it blow over. Do not fill the instant pot more than halfway with beans, grains, one-pot pasta, oat, cornmeal or any other expandables, as these might spill over. Note that pressure cooking level for typical food is maximum 2/3 full, while that for expandable foods like grains and beans is maximum ½ full.

5. Under no circumstances should you try to force open the pressure cooker lid of the instant pot.

6. Always wash the lid, and clean the anti-block shield and inner pot of the instant pot after every use.

7. Ensure that the silicone sealing ring (gasket) is always in good shape and check for any food residue in the anti-block shield before every use.

8. Thickening agents like flour, cornstarch, and condensed soups should not be added before pressure cooking.

9. Ensure that the inner lining of the pot is always present to avoid pouring anything directly on the base of the instant pot.

10. Adhere to the regulatory warnings of the instant pot when in use (burn warning, etc.)

11. Do not place your instant pot on the stovetop or oven to avoid melting, especially if the stovetop is still hot.

12. Take note of other safety mechanisms, as indicated in the instant pot manual.

13. Most importantly, if you notice anybody misusing the instant pot, do not hesitate to say something.

Converting recipes from regular pot to the instant pot

The instant pot comes with much excitement on its uniqueness in preparation of meals. However, there are usually some lingering confusion and concerns as to how to measure the ingredients or convert your usual pot recipe into the instant pot recipe. This is because the instant pot cooks at different temperatures and pressure, and the steam does not escape while cooking. This, therefore, means that the measurement for the ingredients you use when cooking or baking with the normal pot and stove might not necessarily give the same results in an instant pot. You should, therefore, ensure to take specific measures to adapt your recipe to the new environment of the instant pot.

1. Make sure that your recipe works for the instant pot:

This is usually the first problem that most people encounter when using the instant pot. While the instant pot is ideal for most recipes, it is not suitable for every recipe. The good news is that this book comes filled with a lot of delicious recipes that you can easily pull off with your instant pot. As earlier pointed out, the possibilities are seemingly endless with an instant pot. There are enough recipes contained herein to keep your fridge stocked with yummy bakes and dishes of different varieties.

2. Endeavor to Add Liquid as Needed:

If you are not strictly following the instructions on the recipes, endeavor that you stick to the minimum fluid requirements for the instant pot. This is to ensure proper pressurization and get the best results when making some tweaks of your own. There is no harm in experimentation, and there is that unique taste which we all crave from time to time, but always stick to the basics.

Note, however, that you don't have to drown your recipe in water to achieve the instant pressure cooking. You only need to alter the liquid content of your regular pot recipe depending on how long you are cooking.

For pressure cooking, cut the liquid by at least half or even three-quarters, while for slow cooking, decrease the liquid by a third.

3. Altering the Cooking Time:

This is one of the most lauded advantages of the instant pot. As such, it has to be taken into consideration when converting your recipe for use in the instant pot. That meal that usually takes one hour to prepare ordinarily might end up being ready within 30 minutes when prepared using an instant pot. You do not expect to alter the liquid content of your recipe for the instant pot and not reduce the cooking time. If this is not done, you might find yourself seeing the "burn" warning on the instant pot more often than not.

That said, there is no hard and fast rule in altering the cooking time for most of your recipes. Pay more attention to the cooking time for the individual ingredients contained in your recipe as indicated by your instant pot manual. You will find out that you might not necessarily need to "add all ingredients" at the same time as is common with most traditional recipes. This is because some ingredients might take longer to cook than others depending on the mode of your instant pot. If added at the same time, therefore, some ingredients might end up undercooked.

Generally, for pressure cooking, plan for about a third of the average cooking time, while for slow cooking, double or quadruple the standard cooking time.

4. Measuring the Ingredients:

As a general tip, hold off on dairy ingredients when using the instant pot as much as you can. This is because dairy ingredients cook a lot different in the instant pot than on the stove, slow cooker, or the oven. If, however, the recipe calls for the inevitable use of dairy ingredients, then ensure that you add them after you have cooked and depressurized your instant pot. The high pressure and heat of the instant pot can cause dairy products to scorch, leading to a ruined meal.

When converting recipes for the instant pot, be mindful of the size of your pot and endeavor not to get it too filled up. If you are cooking anything that expands (pasta, rice, and even dough during baking), try to scale the recipe back to accommodate for the expansion inside the instant pot. In this case, ensure that your instant pot is not more than half-full during baking.

Quick tips on the effective use of instant pot

Generally;

- Check your valve regularly before cooking to make sure that the pressure release is in the "sealing" position. If in slow cooking mode, set the valve to "venting" position.
- Ignore the initial steam release when the instant pot first begins to pressurize. It is totally normal and should stop once the lid has wholly sealed.
- Get an extra stainless inner pot if you intend to use your instant pot regularly. This will come in handy when you want to cook multiple dishes in succession.

For baking;

- Try getting a pan that will actually fit in the instant pot and keep it out of water.
- You can use a trivet to create a makeshift oven in the instant pot by adding the trivet to the bottom of the instant pot where it acts as an oven rack.
- Remember to line the inside of your baking pan with foil or parchment paper to prevent the barter from sticking inside the instant pot.

Benefits of baking with the instant pot

Apart from the reduced baking time (depending on the mode of cooking) and other afore-mentioned benefits of using the instant pot, other advantages include;

- It helps to keep your kitchen clean.
- Saves not only time but energy also.
- It is very easy to clean up, and the pot as a whole is dishwasher-safe.
- There is no need to defrost food items before cooking or baking.
- Helps in the retention of essential vitamins and nutrients as they are not allowed to escape as steam.
- Preserves food appearance and taste, giving you the perfect results for your recipe.
- It eliminates harmful micro-organisms.
- It comes with a lot of automatic and regulatory mechanisms that always warn you when your meal is not cooking best.
- With the instant pot, there is literally no sweat, no smell, no steam, and no noise.
- Very convenient and arguably affordable.

With all these in mind, there is really nothing stopping you from pulling out your instant pot and baking all the sumptuous recipes contained in this book.

Instant Pot Chocolate Lava Cake

Chocolate lava cake is quite rich and easy to make. The cake can be ready in less than 30 minutes and that makes it worth trying out. The ingredients are also readily available which makes it easy to prepare. This cake is a perfect quick fix for those with chocolate cravings.

Prep Time:	7 minutes	Calories:	622
Cook Time:	10 minutes	Fat (g):	40
Total Time:	17 minutes	Protein (g):	9
Servings:	4	Net carbs (g):	57

Ingredients:

- Dark chocolate chips – 1 cup
- Eggs – 3
- Flour – ¼ cup
- Butter – ½ cup
- Vanilla – 1 teaspoon
- Sugar – ½ cup
- Raspberries - optional
- Mint leaves – optional

Instructions:

1. In a microwave-friendly bowl, add chocolate chips and butter then microwave for about 30 seconds then remove from the microwave once done and stir.
2. In a different bowl, whisk together flour, sugar, vanilla, and eggs then stir until well combined. Pour chocolate mixture into the egg mixture then stir until well combined.
3. Spray about 6 ramekins with cooking spray then fill each with the mixed butter.
4. Place steam rack at the bottom of the instant pot then adds about 2 cups of water. Place the ramekins over the rack then cover the pot and set to sealing.
5. Set time manually to 8 minutes as you set to high pressure.
6. Quick-release once has done then remove the ramekins carefully from the pot. Serve with ice cream, raspberries and mint as garnish.

Peanut butter chocolate cheesecake

This is a beautiful dessert recipe that one can easily prepare. You can add a crust to it by using oreo cookie crumbs and some melted butter. The cake is just delicious and very moist.

Prep Time:	10 minutes	Calories:	352
Cook Time:	35 minutes	Fat (g):	25
Total Time:	45 minutes	Protein (g):	6
Servings:	6	Net carbs (g):	26

Ingredients:

- Cream cheese – 16 ounces
- Eggs – 2
- Smooth peanut butter – ½ cup tablespoons
- Vanilla extract – 1 teaspoon
- Cocoa – 1 teaspoon

Instructions:

1. Add the eggs and cream cheese to the blender then combine until well mixed. Add the remaining ingredients as well then blend until well combined.

2. Place the mixture into a pan then cover with foil. Add 1 cup of water into the instant pot then insert trivet.

3. Place the cake pan into the trivet then cover the instant pot and set to sealing. Let it cook for 40 minutes over high pressure or until done.

4. Release pressure naturally for 5 minutes. Allow chilling overnight then top with oreo crumbs and the melted butter. You can drizzle with peanut butter or even top with chopped peanuts as desired.

Instant Pot Cherry Cobbler

This is an easy to prepare instant pot recipe that's moist and also very delicious. You can alternate the ingredients as you find to be ideal.

Prep Time:	10 minutes	Calories:	184
Cook Time:	30 minutes	**Fat (g):**	6
Total Time:	40 minutes	**Protein (g):**	2
Servings:	4	**Net carbs (g):**	32

Ingredients:

- Cherry Pie filling – 20 ounces can
- Granulated sugar – ¾ cup
- All-purpose flour – ¾ cup
- Vanilla extract – 1 teaspoon
- Melted butter – 6 tablespoon

Instructions:

1. Add a cup of water to the instant pot then place the trivet inside.
2. Get the cake pan greased using cooking spray then pour cherry pie filling into the pan.
3. In a bowl, mix together flour, sugar and salt then drizzle vanilla extract and melted the butter as you mix together until well combined.
4. Squeeze cobbler dough into the mixture then shape it into a round shape.
5. Place the mixture over the cherry pie filling in the pan then cover the pan using a paper towel.
6. Create a foil sling using aluminum foil then use it for lowering the pan into the instant pot.
7. Close the lid of the instant pot to sealing then let it cook on high pressure for about 30 minutes.
8. Quick-release pressure once the cooking time is up then let it stay for about 3 minutes to cool before serving.

Pecan Chocolate Chip Cake

Chocolate chip cake is just so yummy and easy to make. It looks so pretty when taken with some ganache topping. The texture is moist and very delicious with makes it worth trying out. You can also try alternating ingredients for that unique taste.

Prep Time:	10 minutes	Calories:	199
Cook Time:	25 minutes	Fat (g):	7
Total Time:	35 minutes	Protein (g):	3
Servings:	6	Net carbs (g):	33

Ingredients:

- Boxed yellow cake mix – ½ (15.25) oz (with pudding mix)
- Brown sugar – 1 tablespoon
- Vegetable oil – ¼ cup
- Chopped pecans – ½ cup
- Semi-sweet chocolate chips – ½ cup
- Eggs – 2
- Coldwater – ¼ cup

Chocolate topping:

- Semi-sweet chocolate chips – ½ cup
- Chopped pecans – ½ cup

Instructions:

1. Combine all of the ingredients apart from chocolate chips and pecans into a bowl then mix together.
2. Fold the pecans and chocolate chips into the batter then pour the mixture into a greased pan.
3. Cover the pan using a foil and paper towel and seal it completely. Add a cup of water into the instant pot then place trivet. Lower the pan over the trivet then cover the lid and set steam release knob to sealing position.
4. Press pressure cook and set time to 25 minutes. Once the cooking cycle ends, release pressure naturally for about 10 minutes.

5. Open the lid once all pressure is out then gently remove the paper towel and foil from the pan. Check to ensure that the cake is cooked all through then give it some time to cool.

6. Place it on a plate then drizzle with chocolate topping.

7. To prepare chocolate topping, melt the chocolate chips and a tablespoon of heavy cream then stir until well combined.

8. Drizzle the cake with chocolate topping then serve.

Lemon cheesecake

Sweet, tart and sour are the best words that describe this lemon cheesecake. It's such a fantastic dessert that can be easily made using the instant pot. You can alternate the ingredients as desired for a more personalized taste.

Prep Time:	20 minutes	Calories:	352
Cook Time:	35 minutes	Fat (g):	25
Total Time:	55 minutes	Protein (g):	6
Servings:	8	Net carbs (g):	26

Ingredients:

- Cream cheese – 8 oz
- Ricotta cheese – 1/3 cup

- Lemon juice – 1
- Lemon extract – ½ teaspoon
- Eggs – 2
- Lemon zest – 1
- For topping:
- Sour cream – 2 tablespoons
- Truvia – 1 teaspoon

Instructions:

1. Mix all the ingredients together using a stand mixer except the eggs
2. Add the eggs then blend to incorporate the eggs.
3. Pour the mixture into a greased springform then cover with foil
4. Add two cups of water into the inner liner of the instant pot and the trivet then place the covered pot into the trivet.
5. Cook for 30 minutes on high pressure then release pressure naturally once cooked.
6. Mix the sour cream with Truvia then spread over the warm cake
7. Refrigerate for six hours then serve when cool and enjoy

Instant Pot Sourdough Bread

This is such a crusty and delicious bread that's made with yogurt. It takes less than four hours from start to finish to prepare the bread. The bread is also ideal for making sandwiches.

Prep Time:	5 minutes	Calories:	130
Cook Time:	30 minutes	Fat (g):	0
Total Time:	35 minutes	Protein (g):	6
Servings:	8	Net carbs (g):	23

Ingredients:

- Bread flour – 3 cups
- Instant yeast – ¾ teaspoons
- Unflavored Greek Yoghurt – 1 ½ cups
- Salt – 1 ½ teaspoon

Instructions:

1. In a large bowl combine together flour, yeast and salt.
2. Add yogurt to the mixture the combine until dough is formed. If in case the mixture is very dry, add a few teaspoons of yogurt.
3. Form into a ball then line the instant with some parchment paper. Place dough ball into the pot then cover the lid and press yogurt button. Let the dough stay in there for about 4 hours.
4. Remove from the instant pot then place on a floured surface. Knead dough then shape into a ball. Cover it using a tea towel then place in a floured proofer basket and cover.
5. In the meantime, get the dutch pan preheated to about 450^0F for about 30 minutes.
6. Place the dough ball carefully into the dutch pan then cover with a lid.
7. Let it bake for about 25 minutes then remove the lid and allow to bake for another 10 minutes or until well browned.
8. Remove from the oven then allow to cool.

Instant Pot Banana Bread

This is just delicious moist banana bread that melts into the mouth effortlessly. You can alternate the ingredients as desired for a more flavorful bread.

Prep Time:	10 minutes	Calories:	222
Cook Time:	50 minutes	Fat (g):	10
Total Time:	1 hour 20 minutes	Protein (g):	4
Servings:	8	Net carbs (g):	32

Ingredients:

- 3 extra ripe bananas

- All-purpose flour – 1 ½ cups
- Baking soda – 1 teaspoon
- Sugar – ½ cup
- 1 Pinch salt
- Vanilla extract – 1 teaspoon
- Large egg – 1 beaten
- Melted butter – 1/3 cup
- Baking soda – 1 teaspoon

Instructions:

1. Use cooking spray or butter to coat the loaf pan.
2. In a bowl, mash bananas using a fork then add a mixture of vanilla extract, egg and butter.
3. Add in flour then mix ½ cup of flour at a time. Pour the banana bread mixture into the prepared loaf pan then level it out using a spatula.
4. Cover the loaf pan using a paper towel and then add aluminum foil over it.
5. Into the instant pot, add a cup of water then insert trivet. Place the loaf pan that's covered into the pot.
6. Cover with a secure lid as you ensure that it's set to sealing.
7. Turn instant pot to manual then set time to about 50 minutes. Once the timer ends, quick release the valve then remove the loaf pan carefully from the pot and place on a cooling wire rack for about 5 minutes.
8. Remove bread from the loaf pan and let it cool further on the wire rack.
9. Slice and enjoy.

Zucchini Banana Bread

This is such a moist and easy to make bread that combines zucchini and banana so well. The mini chocolate chips are a bonus and take the flavor to a whole new level. You can alternate the recipes as desired for a personalized taste.

Prep Time:	15 minutes	Calories:	422
Cook Time:	60 minutes	Fat (g):	20
Total Time:	1 hour 10 minutes	Protein (g):	8
Servings:	6	Net carbs (g):	55

Ingredients:

- Mashed ripe banana – 2
- Shredded zucchini – 1 small
- Egg- 1
- Coconut oil – ½ cup
- Whole wheat flour – 1 ½ cups
- White vinegar – 1/3 cup
- Baking powder – ½ teaspoon
- Brown sugar – 1/3 cup
- Mini chocolate chips – 1 cup
- Baking soda – 1 teaspoon
- Salt – ½ teaspoon

Instructions:

1. In a bowl whisk mashed banana, egg, oil and zucchini.
2. Stir in flour, sugars, salt, baking powder and whisk together until well combined with no streaks remaining. Avoid over mixing.
3. Prepare a cake pan by spraying with some non-stick cooking spray. Pour the mixture into the pan then cover with foil.
4. Add a cup of water into the instant pot bottom then place trivet into the pot.
5. Place the springform pan over the trivet then use your handles to carefully lower the pan.
6. Cover the pot then press manual button and set the timer to 60 minutes over high pressure. Ensure that the valve is also set to sealing.

7. Once the timer beeps, turn the valve to venting then use hot pads to remove the pan and trivet from the instant pot.
8. Allow the bread to stay for about 10 minutes then remove foil and serve warm or as desired.

Very Vanilla Cheese Cake

This is such a perfect cheesecake that has such a nice texture. Making it using an instant pot helps with preventing the top from cracking which is just great. You can leave it as plain or top as desired.

Prep Time:	25 minutes	Calories:	484
Cook Time:	60 minutes	**Fat (g):**	34
Total Time:	1 hour 25 minutes	**Protein (g):**	8
Servings:	6	**Net carbs (g):**	39

Ingredients:

- Graham cracker crumbs – ¾ cup
- Water – 1 cup
- Ground cinnamon – ¼ teaspoon
- Melted butter – 2 ½ tablespoons
- Softened cream cheese – 2 packages (8 ounces)
- Sugar – 2/3 cup + 1 tablespoon
- Vanilla extract – 3 teaspoons
- Large eggs – lightly beaten

Topping (Optional)

- White baking chocolate – 4 ounces chopped
- Heavy whipping cream – 3 tablespoons
- Fresh raspberries or strawberries (optional)

Instructions:

1. Grease springform then pours water into the instant pot. In a bowl mix together cracker crumbs, cinnamon, a tablespoon of sugar and butter then add to the bottom of the pan.
2. In another bowl, add the remaining sugar then combine with cream cheese and mix until smooth. Add vanilla, eggs and mix until well combined. Pour the mixture over the crust.
3. Cover the cheesecake with a tight foil then place the springform pan on a trivet and lower into the instant pot. Lock the lid and ensure its set to sealed.

4. Select manual setting and set time to one hour. Once the time is up, quick release pressure then allows cooling.

5. The cheesecake should be somehow jiggly but well set in the center. Remove springform pan from the instant pot then place the cheesecake on a wire rack and allow to stay for about 1 hour.

6. Loosen the sides from the pan using a knife then refrigerate overnight as you completely cover.

Instant Pot Maple Toast

This is a perfect bread that is easy to prepare. It takes far much less time when done using instant pot and you can top it up with some powdered sugar and preferred fruit. Maple syrup makes it all better.

Prep Time:	10 minutes	Calories:	378
Cook Time:	20 minutes	Fat (g):	17
Total Time:	30 minutes	Protein (g):	14
Servings:	6	Net carbs (g):	42

Ingredients:

- Cubed bread – 6 cups
- Cream cheese cubed – 4 ounces
- Large eggs – 4
- Milk – ½ cup
- Maple syrup – ¼ cup
- Water – 1 cup
- Maple syrup

Instructions:

1. In a greased baking dish, arrange half of the bread cubes. Top using cream cheese and the remaining bread.
2. In a large bowl, whisk together eggs, syrup and milk then pour over the bread and allow to stay for about 30 minutes.
3. Add water to the bottom of the instant pot then place trivet. Cover the dish with foil then lower into the instant pot.
4. Lock the lid the set to sealing. Adjust to high pressure the set time to 20 minutes.
5. Once cooking is up, release pressure naturally for about 10 minutes then quick release the remaining pressure.
6. Remove the lid then carefully remove the pan from the instant pot.
7. Serve with syrup.

Instant Pot Puerto Rican Flan

This Puerto Rican Flan recipe is just so delicious and quite easy o prepare. You can also prepare it using the oven. You can consider using cream cheese to prepare the cake. You can also add a few ingredients as you find to be ideal.

Prep Time:	10 minutes	Calories:	392
Cook Time:	20 minutes	Fat (g):	17
Total Time:	30 minutes	Protein (g):	15
Servings:	4	Net carbs (g):	45

Ingredients:

- Sweetened condensed milk – 14 ounces
- Evaporated milk – 26 ounces

- Vanilla – 1 tablespoon
- Large eggs – 6
- Sugar – 1 cup
- Water – ½ cup

Instructions:

For the caramel

1. In microwave-safe glassware, add sugar and water then place the container into the microwave and let it cook for about 4 minutes or until the sugar turns into some golden syrup.
2. Pour the mixture of sugar into the baking pot then swirl to ensure that the caramel coats at the bottom of the pan.
3. Set it aside once ready.

To prepare custard

1. Blend the remaining ingredients using a blender then mix until the mixture is creamy for about 3 minutes.
2. Add water into the pot then insert the steam rack.
3. Pour flan mixture into the pan then cover using aluminum foil. Place the pan into the pot then add the lid and close valve.
4. Set instant pot to manual high and set timer to 8 minutes. Release pressure naturally once ready.
5. Remove the pan from inside the pot and refrigerate for about 4 hours.
6. Serve and enjoy.

Fast French Bread

Fast French bread is just magnificent and tastes so good. It's easy to make with the chewy and the outer crust looking so appealing. The chewy inside makes it taste so good. You can alternate the ingredients as desired for the desired flavor however the ones shared are just delicious.

Prep Time:	10 minutes	Calories:	390
Cook Time:	20 minutes	Fat (g):	6
Total Time:	30 minutes	Protein (g):	12
Servings:	8	Net carbs (g):	60

Ingredients:

- Warm water – 2 ½ cups (divided)
- Sugar – 1 ½ tablespoon (divided)
- Cooking oil – 2 tablespoon
- Bread flour – 6 cups
- Quick rise yeast – 1 ½ tablespoon

Instructions:

1. Combine warm water ½ cup with sugar and yeast then allow the mixture to stay for about 10 minutes or until bubbly.
2. Add the mixed bubbly yeast alongside other ingredients and the remaining water to a bowl of a mixer. Use the dough hook then combine together all of the ingredients and allow the mixer to knead for about 5 minutes.
3. Roll the dough into small balls then pour a tablespoon of oil into the instant pot and press the yogurt button. Roll the dough in oil so as not to stick.
4. Divide the dough into small loaves as desired then roll the dough into rectangular shapes as desired. Score the top of the dough with a knife.
5. Get the oven set at 425^0F as you allow the dough to rise until it gets to double as the oven continues to heat.
6. Bake the dough for about 10 minutes then reduce the temperature to about 375^0F.
7. Serve and enjoy

No-knead Instant Pot Bread

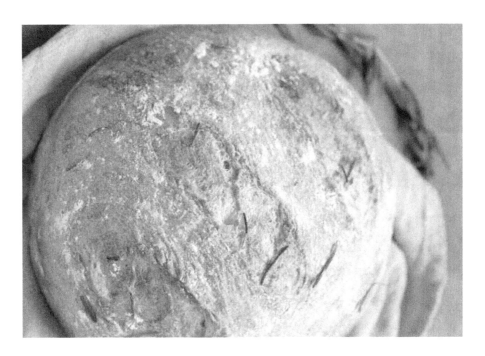

Prep Time:	5 minutes	Calories:	155
Cook Time:	45 minutes	Fat (g):	6
Total Time:	50 minutes	Protein (g):	3
Servings:	12	Net carbs (g):	23

Ingredients:

- Warm water – 1 cup
- Yeast – 1 ¼ teaspoon
- Salt – ½ tablespoons
- Flour – 2 ¼ cups

Instructions:

1. Begin by greasing the cake pan and lining it with parchment paper.

2. Add trivet then pour 1 cup of water. In a bowl, add warm water, salt and yeast then let it stay for about 3 minutes.

3. Add flour into the mixture then combine well until well mixed. Pour the dough into the pan then place inside the instant pot and cover the lid. Press keep warm setting and let the dough stay for about 2 hours.

4. Once the dough has increased in size, cover the instant pot lid and press on manual then set time to about 45 minutes.

5. Release pressure naturally then once the bread is done, toss it under the broiler and let it stay for about 5 minutes for the golden-brown crust to form.

Apple Cinnamon Cake

This is a tender and moist cake that is loaded with rich cinnamon flavor and fresh apples. You can serve it warm as it's quite delicious if taken with some scoop of vanilla. You can also allow it to cool then sprinkle some powdered sugar over the top. You can also alternate the ingredients as desired.

Prep Time:	15 minutes	Calories:	354
Cook Time:	60 minutes	Fat (g):	16
Total Time:	1 hour 15 minutes	Protein (g):	4
Servings:	8	Net carbs (g):	49

Ingredients:

For apples:

- Apples – 2 ½ cups (peeled, cored and diced)
- Ground cinnamon – ½ tablespoon
- Granulated sugar – 2 tablespoons

Cake:

- Baking powder – ½ tablespoon
- Flour – 1 ½ cups
- Vegetable oil – ½ cup
- Sugar – ¾ cup
- Orange juice – 2 tablespoons
- Large eggs – 2
- Sea salt – ½ teaspoon
- Water – 1 cup
- Powdered sugar – for decorating the cake.

Instructions:

1. In a bowl mix together all of the dry ingredients then set aside.
2. In a different bowl, combine the wet ingredients then once mixed add the dry ingredients and combine well.
3. Grease the cake pan then pour the mixture into the pan. Spread half of the apples over the butter mixture.
4. Add some more butter to cover the apple pieces then spread the apples and the juices over the top.

5. Cover the cake pan with aluminum foil.

6. Add water into the instant pot then place the wrapped cake pan on the trivet and into the instant pot.

7. Press manual as you set the pressure to high then set time to 60 minutes. Once done, release pressure naturally before opening the pot.

8. Remove the wrapped cake from the trivet then allow to cool for about 15 minutes.

9. Sprinkle the cake with powdered sugar then serve warm and enjoy.

Vegan Chocolate Cake

Instant pot makes it possible to take cake baking to a whole new level. This vegan chocolate cake is just so delicious and ideal for anyone craving some chocolate. The cake is easy to make, moist and also very fluffy which is just amazing.

Prep Time:	10 minutes	Calories:	326
Cook Time:	40 minutes	Fat (g):	19
Total Time:	50 minutes	Protein (g):	5
Servings:	12	Net carbs (g):	53

Ingredients:

- All-purpose flour – ¾ cup
- Vegan sugar of choice – ½ cup
- Unsweetened cocoa powder – ½ cup
- Baking powder – ½ teaspoon
- Nut or plant milk – ½ cup
- Baking soda – ½ teaspoon
- Vanilla extract – ½ teaspoon
- Apple cider vinegar – 1 teaspoon
- Sweet chocolate chips
- Cooking oil – ¼ cup

Instructions:

1. Coat the baking pan with oil and parchment paper then set it aside.
2. Mix all of the dry ingredients in a bowl then combine well and set aside.
3. Combine all of the liquids in a separate bowl then whisk together until well melted and combined.
4. Pour the mixture of liquids over the dry ones then whip together using a spatula.
5. Pour the mixed batter into the prepared pan then cover the pan with foil. Place the baking pan inside the instant pot after adding a cup of water at the base and trivet.
6. Cover the instant pot and set to sealing then allow to bake under high pressure for about 40 minutes.

7. Check the level of doneness by inserting a toothpick at the center. It should come out clean.

8. Release pressure naturally then allows it to cool for about 10 minutes.

9. Place the cake on a cooling wire rack then serve and enjoy as desired.

Cinnamon Roll French Toast Casserole

This is a very delicious breakfast dish that's also very filling. It is completely made using the instant pot. You can make it as a meal prep breakfast recipe that will be loved by both family and friends.

Prep Time:	15 minutes	Calories:	368
Cook Time:	25 minutes	Fat (g):	17
Total Time:	40 minutes	Protein (g):	9
Servings:	6	Net carbs (g):	37

Ingredients:

- Sourdough bread that's sliced into small cubes.
- Large eggs – 8
- Milk – 1 cup
- Maple extract – 2 tablespoons
- Chopped walnuts – ½ cups

For the almond cinnamon drizzle

- Drippy almond butter – 2/3 cup
- Maple syrup – 2 tablespoons
- Melted coconut oil

Optional topping

- Chilled butter – 4 tablespoons
- Brown sugar – ¼ cup

Instructions:

1. Spray a glass bowl using coconut spray then set aside.
2. In a different bowl mix together all of the ingredients for almond butter cinnamon drizzle.
3. In a different bowl, whisk together maple syrup, vanilla, eggs and milk. Place half of the bread cubes and the walnuts into the prepared glass bowl then drizzle with the almond butter cinnamon drizzle.
4. Add the remaining bread cubes and the walnuts then sprinkle again over the bread.

5. Pour the egg mixture over the mixed bread cubes then combine together using a spatula.

6. Sprinkle with your preferred topping the insert instant pot trivet into the instant pot then pour cup water at the bottom of the pot.

7. Lock the instant pot then turn the valve to sealing. Press on manual then turn to high pressure and allow to cook for about 25 minutes.

8. Then quick-release pressure.

9. Allow to cool then serve with maple syrup and fruit.

Churros Muffins

These homemade churros are quite delicious and moist. The taste somehow exists between a muffin and a donut and that makes them worth trying out. The yummy muffins can be turned to vegan-friendly bites with a little bit of substituting butter for the vegan butter. You can adjust the ingredients to that which appeals to you best.

Prep Time:	5 minutes	Calories:	89
Cook Time:	20 minutes	Fat (g):	4
Total Time:	25 minutes	Protein (g):	0
Servings:	24	Net carbs (g):	12

Ingredients:

- Organic coconut sugar – 1/3 cup
- Cinnamon powder – 1 teaspoon
- Dairy-free milk – ½ cup
- Whole wheat – 1 cup
- Melted butter ¼ cup
- Ground cinnamon – 2 tablespoons
- White sugar – ½ cup
- Baking powder – 1 teaspoon
- Unsalted butter

Instructions:

1. In a bowl add melted butter, cinnamon powder, sugar, and milk then stir until well combined.
2. Add baking powder and flour to the mixture then stir well to combine. Grease the egg bite molds then fill with the mixture until half full.
3. Cover the egg bite mold using aluminum foil then place in a trivet. Add a cup of water into then insert the trivet and cover the pot.
4. Then choose the "Cake" setting (10 minutes) . Choose quick release for temperature.
5. Once the time is up, remove the foil then place a plate on the tray and flip it to slide to the right.
6. Remove from the instant pot once done. To coat the churros, melt butter in a bowl then in a separate bowl, mix together cinnamon with sugar.

7. Remove the churro bites from the pan then dip each of the bites into the melted butter. Roll each into the mixture then allow to cool and serve.

Fluffy Pancake Cinnamon Rolls

Fluffy pancake is tasty and delicious rolls that are worth trying out. You can use the preferred toppings. The ingredients are quite easily available and that makes the recipe worth trying out. You can also substitute the ingredients as desired for a more personalized look.

Prep Time:	10 minutes	Calories:	464
Cook Time:	20 minutes	Fat (g):	24
Total Time:	30 minutes	Protein (g):	11
Servings:	6	Net carbs (g):	56

Ingredients:

Dough mixture:

- Pancake mix – 1 ¼ cup
- Milk – 1/3 cup
- Sugar – 1 tablespoon

Filling mixture:

- Softened butter – 1 tablespoon
- Cinnamon – ½ teaspoon
- Brown sugar – 2 tablespoon

Icing mixture:

- Powdered sugar – ½ cup
- Vanilla – ¼ teaspoon
- Milk – 1 tablespoon

Instructions:

1. In a bowl, mix the dough mixture using a fork until combined.
2. Roll the dough into a rectangle of 4 x 9 inches.
3. In a separate bowl, combine the filling mixture ingredients then spread it evenly over the dough.
4. Roll the dough up right from the short side then cut into about 6 equal slices.
5. Add a cup of water into the instant pot then add the trivet. Place the baking pan carefully over the trivet. Cover the lid as you ensure the vent is closed.

6. Choose manual function then set the time to 12 minutes. Once the time is up, quick release pressure then removes the pan from inside the pot. Set the pan under the broiler and cook for about 5 minutes until golden.

7. In a different bowl, add icing mixture ingredients then drizzle over the rolls while still warm

8. Serve immediately.

Homemade Pancakes with Blueberries

You will require some silicone mold for making this recipe. You can also come up with some new ways that you can use to make the pancakes. If in case you are using more batter then you can add the cooking time appropriately. The pancakes are just so delicious and worth trying out.

Prep Time:	5 minutes	Calories:	137
Cook Time:	20 minutes	Fat (g):	3
Total Time:	25 minutes	Protein (g):	3
Servings:	3	Net carbs (g):	23

Ingredients:

- All-purpose flour – 1 cup
- Sugar – ½ tablespoon
- Milk – ¾ cup
- Egg – 1
- Melted butter – 1 tablespoon
- Maple syrup and blueberries
- Baking powder – 1 teaspoon

Instructions:

1. In a bowl, mix together sugar, flour, baking powder and salt.
2. In a different bowl, whisk the eggs then add milk and butter. You can add about 1 tablespoon of maple syrup if desired.
3. Add the wet mixture to the dry ones until well combined and without lumps. Fold the blueberries gently then divide the mixture equally into silicone tray.
4. Cover silicone tray with some paper towel then covers it up with aluminum foil. Add a cup of water into the pot then add the metal trivet into the pot. Place the foil-covered tray over the trivet then cover the lid and set the valve to sealing.
5. Press cake button then set time to five minutes. Set natural pressure release for 3 minutes once ready then quick release the remaining pressure.
6. Remove the tray from the pan then turn it out onto a flat surface
7. Serve it with maple syrup, butter and some blueberries as desired.

Whole Grain Pancake Muffins

This is a classic whole-grain pancake that's very delicious and worth trying out. The pancake is soft and quite yummy. You can alternate the ingredients as desired as long as it doesn't completely alter the recipe.

Prep Time:	6 minutes	Calories:	190
Cook Time:	15 minutes	Fat (g):	2
Total Time:	21 minutes	Protein (g):	14
Servings:	4	Net carbs (g):	30

Ingredients:

- Waffle mix and kodiak flapjack– 2 cups (any flavor)
- Water – 2 cups

Instructions:

1. In a bowl, combine together Kodiak flapjack and waffle mix as per the stated instructions.
2. Spray the silicone molds with nonstick spray. Use an ice cream scoop to divide the batter in the molds. Place one of the molds over the trivet.
3. Place some 4 narrow mason jar lids over the silicone mold. Add one cup of water into the instant pot then place trivet into the pot.
4. Secure the lid then turn the valve into sealed position. Cook it at high pressure for about 5 minutes. Once the time is up, release pressure naturally for about 5 minutes and then let off the remaining pressure.
5. Allow the pancake bites time to cool. You can enjoy them warm or with some side syrup or honey dipping.
6. Refrigerate the remaining for later use.

Orange Chocolate Cake

This is one of those yummy cakes that you can experiment making with the instant pot. The orange chocolate cake is just delicious with the flavors well balanced. You can alternate the ingredients as desired for that magnificent taste.

Prep Time:	10 minutes	Calories:	362
Cook Time:	25 minutes	Fat (g):	6
Total Time:	35 minutes	Protein (g):	15
Servings:	4	Net carbs (g):	45

Ingredients:

- Salted butter – 6 tablespoons (cubed)
- Egg yolks – 6
- Egg whites – 6
- Sugar – ½ cup
- Fresh orange zest – 2 tablespoons

Instructions:

1. Grease springform pan with coating oil then set aside.
2. In a bowl, add chocolate and butter then melt in a microwave for about 15 seconds. Once completely melted, add the egg yolks, orange zest to the chocolate mixture then stir until well combined.
3. In another bowl, whisk the egg whites using a handheld mixer until foamy and white then add sugar as you continue whisking.
4. Fold the egg white mixture gently into the chocolate mixture then stir until well combined. Pour the mixture into the greased springform pan then add a cup of water into the instant pot.
5. Cover the springform with foil then close the instant pot and cook the cake for about 35 minutes on high pressure.
6. Once the time is up, release pressure naturally then set the cake aside to completely cool.
7. While the cake is cooling, mix together orange extract and heavy cream into a bowl together with powdered sugar until well combined and firm.
8. Use the mixture to top the cake then serve and enjoy.

Lime Pie

This creamy lime pie only takes a few minutes to prepare when using the instant pot. The pie is so delicious and quite satisfying to the sweet tooth. All that you need to prepare this are a few ingredients and you're good to go. If you like tangier flavors then this is just ideal.

Prep Time:	10 minutes	Calories:	172
Cook Time:	15 minutes	Fat (g):	11
Total Time:	25 minutes	Protein (g):	5
Servings:	8	Net carbs (g):	14

Ingredients:

- Vanilla cookies or graham crackers
- Unsalted butter melted.

For the Lime filling:

- Egg yolks – 3 large
- Key lime juice – 2/3 cup
- Lime zest – 1 tablespoon
- Unsweetened condensed milk – 2 tablespoons

Topping (optional)

- Heavy cream – ½ cup
- Sugar – ¼ cup
- Lime zest – 1 teaspoon

Instructions:

1. Spray the springform pan with nonstick spray and use the food processor to grind the crackers.
2. In a bowl, mix together cracker crumbs with melted butter. Press the mixture into the bowl then freeze as you make the filling.
3. Place sugar and the egg yolks into a bowl then use a mixer to combine it well. Add condensed milk to the mixture alongside lime juice and zest then mix until well combined.

4. Pour the mixture over the prepared crust then cover the pan with aluminum foil. Add a cup of water into the instant pot then ad trivet to it. Add the covered pan over the trivet then seal the pot.

5. Cook on manual high pressure with time set to 15 minutes. Allow the pie to cool for about 10 minutes before releasing pressure naturally.

6. Remove pie from the pot then allow to cool and refrigerate for about 4 hours.

7. For the topping, in a bowl whip cream as you slowly add sugar while mixing until it becomes stiff. Pipe it over the pie as you also decorate with zest.

8. Serve and enjoy.

Salted Caramel Cheesecake

Such a creamy and delicious cheesecake that can be easily made with the instant pot. The ingredients can be alternated as desired for an appealing flavor and taste. The cake is moist and also yummy. You can also alternate the toppings as desired.

Prep Time:	20 minutes	Calories:	455
Cook Time:	35 minutes	Fat (g):	32
Total Time:	55 minutes	Protein (g):	7
Servings:	8	Net carbs (g):	36

Ingredients:

For crust:

- Melted butter – 4 tablespoons
- Sugar – 2 tablespoons
- Finely crushed ritz – 1 ½ cups

Cheesecake fillings:

- Cream cheese – 16 ounces
- Light brown sugar – ½ cup
- Sour cream – ¼ cup
- Flour – 1 tablespoon
- Vanilla – 1 ½ teaspoon
- Kosher salt – 1 ½ teaspoon
- Eggs – 2

Topping:

- Caramel sauce – ½ cup
- Flaked sea salt – 1 teaspoon

Instructions:

1. Use cooking spray to spray a7-inch springform and cover the bottom with parchment paper as well.
2. In a bowl, mix together ritz crumbs with sugar and butter evenly. Press the mixture at the bottom firmly then set aside.

3. In a different bowl, mix cream cheese and sugar until well combined then add sour cream and mix for 30 seconds more until smooth. Add flour, vanilla and salt then mix well. Add in the eggs and mix until smooth.

4. Pour cream cheese mixture over the prepared crust. Add 2 cups of water into the instant pot then add trivet into the pot. Cover the springform with a paper towel and aluminum foil

5. Place the covered pan into the instant pot then secure the lid and set to sealing. Adjust pressure to high and set timer to 35 minutes. Let the cheesecake cook then release pressure naturally once done.

6. Remove from the pot once ready then place on a wire rack and allow to cool for about an hour. Cover the cheesecake then refrigerate for about 4 hours.

7. When ready, serve with caramel sauce and a sprinkle of sea salt.

Rice Pudding

This instant pot rice pudding is creamy an also aromatic. It's flavored with nutmeg, cinnamon and a range of ingredients that makes it so flavorful. The pudding is just ready in less than 30 minutes which makes it easy to prepare and worth trying out.

Prep Time:	5 minutes	**Calories:**	178
Cook Time:	20 minutes	**Fat (g):**	3
Total Time:	25 minutes	**Protein (g):**	4
Servings:	8	**Net carbs (g):**	34

Ingredients:

- Whole milk – 2 cups
- Long grained rice – 1 cup
- Water – 1 ¼ cups
- Vanilla extract – 1 teaspoon
- Nutmeg – ½ teaspoon
- Sweetened condensed milk – 1 can
- Pinch of salt

Instructions:

1. Rinse rice well then drain using a fine mesh colander. Add water, milk, cinnamon and nutmeg into the instant pot.
2. Add rice to the pot then stir to combine. Cover the pot with a lid then set to sealing.
3. Press on porridge button then set to cook for about 20 minutes.
4. Once done, release pressure naturally for 10 minutes then cancel to turn off the pot.
5. Open the lid once all the pressure is out then add vanilla extract and sweetened condensed milk.
6. Stir well until fully combined and also creamy.
7. Serve and enjoy

Molten Brownie Pudding

Molten brownie pudding is so yummy and can be served with a scoop of some vanilla ice cream. The recipe is quite ideal for those with chocolate craving and you can alternate the ingredients as desired for that unique taste.

Prep Time:	10 minutes	Calories:	280
Cook Time:	30 minutes	Fat (g):	13
Total Time:	40 minutes	Protein (g):	2
Servings:	4	Net carbs (g):	36

Ingredients:

- Semisweet chocolate chips – ¼ cup
- Vanilla – 1 teaspoon
- Milk chocolate chips – ¼ cup
- Flour – ¼ cup
- Eggs – 2
- Sugar – 1 cup
- Melted butter – 7 tablespoons
- Water – 1 ½ cups
- Salt – 1/8 teaspoon

Instructions:

1. Pour 1 ½ of water into the pot then place the steam rack into the pot. Grease the baking dish with butter.
2. In a bowl, add eggs and sugar then mix until fluffy. In a different bowl, and flour, salt and chocolate chips then mix and add to the sugar and eggs mixture. Combine well until blended. Add in vanilla, melted butter and mix well.
3. Pour the mixture into the prepared dish then sprinkle with chocolate chips. Place the dish over the steam rack then secure the lid.
4. Select temperature to manual then cooks on high pressure for about 30 minutes. Once cooking is complete, release pressure then removes the lid.
5. Remove the baking dish from the pot then allow it to cool for about 5 minutes. Serve with some scoop of vanilla ice cream as desired.

Hazelnut Flan

Hazelnut flan is easy to prepare and can be ready within a short time. The ingredients are easily available and that makes this moist and yummy recipe worth trying out. You can top it with chopped hazelnuts and whipped cream for enhanced flavor taste.

Prep Time:	10 minutes	Calories:	170
Cook Time:	30 minutes	Fat (g):	12
Total Time:	40 minutes	Protein (g):	5
Servings:	6	Net carbs (g):	23

Ingredients:

- Granulated sugar – ¾ cup
- Whole eggs – 3
- Egg yolks – 2
- Granulated sugar – 1/3 cup
- Whole milk – 2 cups
- Vanilla extract – 1 teaspoon
- Hazelnut syrup – 2 tablespoons
- Water – ¼ cup
- Whipping cream – ½ cup
- Pinch of salt

Instructions:

Caramel:

1. Place a saucepan over medium heat then add sugar3/4 cup and water. Bring to boil then cover for about 2 minutes. Remove the cover then continue with the cooking until the mixture becomes amber.
2. Pour the mixture into ungreased custard cups then set aside.

Custard:

1. In a bowl, whisk egg yolks, a pinch of salt and sugar together. Place a saucepan over medium heat the milk until it bubbles. Add the hot milk to the eggs then whisk into the mixture hazelnut syrup, cream and vanilla.
2. Strain it into a measuring bowl then pour a cup of water into the instant pot and add trivet into the pot.

3. Pour custard into the cups then cover with foil and place over trivet inside the instant pot. Stack cups into a layer then lock the lid and select to cook under high pressure. Set time to six minutes then once it beeps release pressure naturally for about 10 minutes.

4. Remove the cups carefully then place on a wire rack and allow to cool uncovered. Once cool, refrigerate for about 4 hours then serve topped with chopped hazelnuts and whipped cream.

Mango Cheesecake

This is such an easy to prepare cheesecake that turns out delicious. It's simple yet very delicious. Remember not to over mix batter as you prepare the cake. Over mixing will create room for the air bubbles in the cake. It's better taken when cooled and chilled.

Prep Time:	10 minutes	Calories:	201
Cook Time:	30 minutes	Fat (g):	14
Total Time:	40 minutes	Protein (g):	4
Servings:	8	Net carbs (g):	20

Ingredients:

- Shelled pistachio – ¾ cup
- Butter melted – 2 tablespoons
- Ground cardamom – ½ teaspoon
- Cream cheese – 8 oz
- Cane sugar – 1/3 cup
- Saffron strands – 8 (soaked in warm water)
- Egg – 1
- Cornstarch – 1 tablespoon
- Mango puree – 1/4cup
- Confectioners sugar – ¼ cup

Instructions:

1. To prepare crust, pulse together cardamom and pistachio in a food processor then combine with sugar, butter and pistachio crumbs.
2. Pour the mixture into a greased springform then line with a parchment paper round.
3. Place the pan inside a freezer while working on the filling.
4. To prepare mango puree, take a cup of frozen mango chunks and thaw. Puree it to get at least ¾ cup of mango puree.
5. In a bowl, beat cream cheese until fluffy for about 45 seconds then add an egg and blend for about 30 seconds.
6. Spread the filling evenly using a spatula then cover the pan with aluminum foil.

7. Pour a cup of water into the pressure cooker then place cake pan over the trivet and add to the instant pot. Set to cook under high pressure for about 30 minutes.
8. Release pressure naturally once cooked. Remove from the instant pot then allow to cool for about 1 hour.
9. To prepare the topping, whisk together the mixture of mango puree and confectioners sugar then pour over the cake so as to evenly spread.

Tip: Refrigerate it overnight before serving.

Crème Brulee

This crème brulee will beautifully melt into your mouth as you consume it. All it takes to make it is just 5 simple ingredients that are readily available. The aroma is also quite satisfying and makes it worth trying out.

Prep Time:	15 minutes	Calories:	382
Cook Time:	35 minutes	Fat (g):	34
Total Time:	50 minutes	Protein (g):	4
Servings:	6	Net carbs (g):	15

Ingredients:

- Heavy cream – 2 cups
- Granulated sugar – 6 tablespoons
- Vanilla extract 1 ¼ teaspoon
- Pinch of salt
- Egg yolks – 6
- Granulated sugar – ¾ teaspoon

Instructions:

1. Begin by separating egg whites from the egg yolks into two different bowls.
2. Place the egg whites into the refrigerator. Warm the cream mixture then add heavy cream, vanilla extract and pinch of salt. Warm the mixture over medium heat as you occasionally stir then set aside.
3. Add to the egg yolks granulated sugar then mix well. Combine the warmed cream with egg yolks then mix well. Combine with the cream mixture then pour into 6 6 oz ramekins. Remove the air bubbles then wrap the ramekins with aluminum foil.
4. Add a cup of water into the instant pot then place the ramekins over steamer rack. Set to cook for 13 minutes over low pressure.
5. Release pressure naturally for about 15 minutes. Remove the ramekins off the instant pot then check if ready.
6. Place the ramekins over a cooling rack then once cooled, refrigerate for about 4 hours.

7. Once ready, serve by spreading ¾ teaspoon of granulated sugar over the cream custard. Caramelize it to form a crispy top.

Fudgy Brownies

Fudgy brownie is one of the go-to recipes that's worth preparing any time. The recipe is easy to make and the ingredients are also readily available. It bakes in standard time and also quite delicious. If you want your brownie moist, super fudgy and chewy ten you can try out this recipe.

Prep Time:	5 minutes	Calories:	380
Cook Time:	50 minutes	Fat (g):	18
Total Time:	55 minutes	Protein (g):	2
Servings:	8	Net carbs (g):	44

Ingredients:

- Brownie mix – 1
- Eggs – 2 large
- Butter – 1 stick

Instructions:

1. In a microwave-safe bowl, melt butter then add two large eggs and blend well. Add brownie mix then mix using a spatula. Grease the baking pan then line with parchment paper.

2. Pour a cup of water into the pan then add trivet and place cake over the top of the trivet.

3. Cover the pan loosely using foil and parchment paper then place the wrapped pan over the trivet. Close the pot then select cake button and press start. Set the vent to sealing the press to cook under high pressure for 40 minutes.

4. Once the time is up, release pressure naturally then let it cool for about 10 minutes.

5. Remove from the pot and also remove foil. Let it cool for 10 more minutes before serving.

Mini White Chocolate Cherry Cakes

This is a simple chocolate cherry cake that's easy to make yet very delicious. The cake is so moist ad yummy with the simple blend of vanilla enhancing the overall taste. You can add an extra pop to the cake with the juicy cherries which are quite delicious.

Prep Time:	15 minutes	Calories:	765
Cook Time:	25 minutes	Fat (g):	45
Total Time:	40 minutes	Protein (g):	8
Servings:	4	Net carbs (g):	81

Ingredients:

- Unsalted butter – 5 tablespoons
- All-purpose flour – ½ cup
- Baking powder – ½ teaspoon
- Baking soda – 1/8 teaspoon
- Granulated sugar – 1/3 cup
- Vanilla extract – 1 teaspoon
- Almond extract – ¼ teaspoon
- White chocolate – 2 oz
- Sour cream – ¼ cup
- Maraschino cherries – 1 oz
- Egg – 1
- Pinch kosher salt

Instructions:

1. Add a cup of water into the instant pot then place the trivet inside. Grease the cake pan with butter then set aside.
2. In a bowl, add butter and sugar then blend until fluffy. Bea in the egg then add almond extract, and vanilla into the pot then mix until well corporated. Add half of the melted chocolate into the bowl then combine with the mixture.
3. Add in flour mixture then combine well with sour cream until well blended.
4. Toss chopped cherries into the mixture then fold gently. Pour the batter into the prepared pans then cover using aluminum foil.

5. Place the pans over trivet in the instant pot then close the lid and set to cook on high pressure for about 25 minutes.

6. Quick-release pressure then removes the lid. Transfer the pans to a rack then allow to cool for about 10 minutes.

7. Serve the cake on dessert plates as you drizzle with the remaining melted white chocolate and also garnish with maraschino cherries.

French Apple Cobbler

If you are in the mood for some dessert then this is quite a perfect choice as its very delicious. You can add all of the ingredients into a bowl and just let it set nicely in a few minutes. The dessert is fruity, creamy and also full of flavor.

Prep Time:	25 minutes	Calories:	275
Cook Time:	35 minutes	Fat (g):	14
Total Time:	60 minutes	Protein (g):	2
Servings:	8	Net carbs (g):	35

Ingredients:

Apple Mixture:

- Sliced apples – 4 cups
- Gluten-free four – 2 tablespoons
- Nutmeg – ¼ teaspoon
- Cinnamon – ½ teaspoon
- Vanilla 1 teaspoon
- Coconut sugar – ½ teaspoon
- Water – ¼ cup
- Sea salt – ½ teaspoon

Cobbler

- Gluten-free flour – ¾ cup
- Coconut sugar – ¼ cup
- Baking powder – ½ teaspoon
- Applesauce – 4 oz
- Seasalt – 1 teaspoon
- Baking soda – ½ teaspoon

Instructions:

1. In a bowl, mix all of the ingredients for apple mixture. The bowl should be that which fits well in the instant pot.
2. In a different bowl, mix the ingredients for cobbler topping. Spoon cobbler mix over the apple mixture.

3. Add a cup of water into the instant pot then place the bowl over the rack and into the pot.

4. Cover the pot then cook for 25 minutes under high pressure. You can release pressure naturally once ready.

5. Remove the bowl from the rack carefully. You can then place it under the broiler if you want a crispy top.

Soda Cake

Such a simple soda cake with the colorful soda giving it such an appealing outlook and taste. If you are looking for something that's easy to make and also delicious then this is quite ideal. You can alternate the ingredients for the desired flavors.

Prep Time:	5 minutes	Calories:	243
Cook Time:	45 minutes	Fat (g):	8
Total Time:	50 minutes	Protein (g):	13
Servings:	6	Net carbs (g):	34

Ingredients:

- Orange cake mix - 1 box
- Orange soda – 12 ounces
- Vanilla ice cream (optional)
- Powdered sugar

Instructions:

1. Grease the pan with nonstick cooking spray then set aside.
2. In a bowl, mix together cake mix with soda until well combined. Pour the mixture into the prepared pan.
3. Cover the pan with a paper towel and foil then wrap loosely with foil.
4. Add a cup of water into the instant pot then add the trivet to the pot. Place the pan over the trivet and tuck foil down into the pan.
5. Cover instant pot then set the valve to sealing. Set it to cook manually over high pressure and set the timer to 45 minutes. Once the cooking time is up, open pressure valve then quick-release pressure.
6. Place the pan on a flat surface then remove foil and the paper towel. Allow it to stay until properly cooled.
7. Place the cake over a serving platter then sprinkle with vanilla ice cream and powdered sugar before serving.

Sticky Toffee Pudding

This is a fabulous instant pot dessert. It's so moist and also very delicious. You can alternate the ingredients as desired for your preferred taste. If you love it to be more exotic then use of dates and caramel is just ideal. Apart from being a bit sticky, it's warm and moist which makes it quite ideal.

Prep Time:	15 minutes	Calories:	242
Cook Time:	25 minutes	Fat (g):	10
Total Time:	40 minutes	Protein (g):	4
Servings:	6	Net carbs (g):	30

Ingredients:

- Chopped dates – ½ cup
- Baking soda – ½ teaspoon
- Bourbon – 2 tablespoons
- Unsalted butter – 3 tablespoons
- Milk – tablespoons
- Baking powder – 1 teaspoon
- Cloves – 1/8 teaspoon
- Cinnamon – ½ teaspoon
- Flour – 2/3 cup
- Egg – 1
- Caramel sauce – ½ cup
- Salt – ¼ teaspoon
- Allspice – 1/8 teaspoon
- Hot water – 6 tablespoons

Instructions:

1. In a small bowl, chop dates into pieces then add to the bowl. Add hot water, bourbon, and baking soda then stir well to combine and set aside.
2. Remove bowl from the microwave then add spices, flour, spices, baking powder and salt then stir to combine.
3. Beat egg into a bowl then add to flour mixture. Add the water and dates mixture then stir all of the ingredients together.
4. Spray 4 ramekins using nonstick spray then divide the mixture into the 4 ramekins. Use foil to cover the ramekins.

5. Place a wire rack into the pot then add ramekins over the wire. Pour 4 cups of water into the instant pot then cover the lid and set to steam. Set time to 25 minutes then release pressure naturally once the time is up.

6. Allow to cool then remove the ramekins from the pot. Set them on some dessert plates then drizzle with caramel sauce. Serve and enjoy.

Lemon Pudding

This is a gluten-free recipe that can be enjoyed by those on dietary restrictions as well. The custard is made using cream, milk or egg yolk. It's very delicious and can be quite filling like a pie or even very thin as a sauce. You can also add the desired flavors for that desired taste.

Prep Time:	20 minutes	Calories:	417
Cook Time:	5 minutes	Fat (g):	12
Total Time:	25 minutes	Protein (g):	9
Servings:	4	Net carbs (g):	45

Ingredients:

- Whole milk – 2 ½ cup
- Cornstarch – 1/3 cup
- Sugar – 1 cup
- Lemon zest- 1 tablespoon
- Eggs – 2
- Egg yolks – 2
- Salt – ¼ teaspoon
- Butter - a tablespoon
- Lemon juice – ¼ cup

Instructions:

1. Place a saucepan over medium heat then add milk, cornstarch, lemon zest, sugar and salt. Bring the mixture to boil as you occasionally stir. Remove from heat once it boils then set aside.

2. Combine the egg whites with egg yolks in a bowl then add lemon custard mixture as you consistently stir.

3. Whisk in butter then allow to melt. Add lemon juice and stir until creamy and smooth. Pour the batter equally into 4 80ounce ramekins as you leave some space on top. Cover each of the ramekins with aluminum foil.

4. Place trivet into the instant pot then adds about 2 cups of water. Place ramekins over the trivet then cover the pot and set the valve to sealing. Set to manual on high pressure and tome to 5 minutes.

5. Once the time is up, carry out a quick release as you turn the pot off. Allow the ramekins to cool then refrigerate for about 2 hours before serving.

Peanut Butter Stuffed Brownie

This brownie is fudgy and also quite delicious. The addition of peanut butter takes it to a whole new level which is just great. If you are not a fun of peanut butter then you can still use it without peanut butter.

Prep Time:	10 minutes	Calories:	317
Cook Time:	50 minutes	Fat (g):	12
Total Time:	60 minutes	Protein (g):	4
Servings:	6	Net carbs (g):	48

Ingredients:

- Softened or melted butter – 5 tablespoon
- Unsweetened cocoa powder – ¼ cup
- Flour – ¾ cup
- Vanilla – ¼ tablespoon
- Sugar – 1 cup
- Eggs – 2
- Creamy peanut butter – 1 tablespoon (optional)
- Diced walnuts optional
- Baking powder – ¾ teaspoon
- Eggs – 2

Instructions:

1. Add all of the dry ingredients into one bowl and the wet ones into a different bowl. You can then stir to combine well.
2. If adding nuts, fold them into the brownie mixture. Spray springform pan with non-stick spray then set aside.
3. Lay parchment paper into the pan then adds caramel pieces in the middle or peanut butter.
4. Pour brownie batter over the top then spread for same thickness all over the pan. Cover it with aluminum foil. Place trivet into the pot then adds a cup of water inside the pot. Place the springform pan over the trivet then cover the instant pot to sealing. Set to manual at high pressure and set a timer to 50 minutes.
5. Do slow release once the time is up then allowed to completely cool

6. Remove the pan from inside the pot then remove foil and parchment paper.

7. Serve when cool and enjoy.

Peach Cobbler

This is an easy to prepare instant pot recipe and all that you need for this delicious recipe is a cake mix and fresh peaches. The recipe looks delicious and takes such a short time to prepare. Fresh peaches are the best to use for this recipe.

Prep Time:	10 minutes	Calories:	482
Cook Time:	10 minutes	Fat (g):	4
Total Time:	20 minutes	Protein (g):	4
Servings:	4	Net carbs (g):	107

Ingredients:

- White cake mix – one box (15.25 oz)
- Softened butter – ¼ cup
- Peaches peeled and also sliced (6 -8) medium)

Instructions:

1. Combine half of the butter and box of cake mix in a bowl then use a pastry blender to cut butter into the mix until evenly crumbled.
2. Place sliced peaches into some oven-safe bowl that can fit inside the pot. Sprinkle cake mix over the peaches.
3. Place foil over the top of the bowl. Insert trivet into the instant pot then place the bowl over the trivet. Pour a cup of water into the pot and cover as you set valve to sealing. Set it on manual with cooking time at 10 minutes on high pressure.
4. Once it beeps, release pressure naturally for 10 minutes. You can then quick-release pressure.
5. Remove the lid then remove the bowl and place under broiler setting for 4 minutes.
6. Serve peach cobbler with some whipped cream or vanilla ice cream.

Pumpkin Pie with Jaggery Crust

Jaggery is a well known traditional sweetener that's made using sugarcane juice. It has a richer taste of sugar and that adds such a tasty touch to the traditional pumpkin pie.

Prep Time:	10 minutes	Calories:	59
Cook Time:	50 minutes	Fat (g):	6
Total Time:	60 minutes	Protein (g):	1
Servings:	10	Net carbs (g):	4

Ingredients:

For jaggery:

- Ghee or butter – 2 tablespoons
- Jaggery – 2 tablespoons
- Almond flour – 1 cup

Ingredients:

- Pumpkin puree – 1 cup
- Maple syrup – ½ cup
- Egg – 1
- Orange zest – 1
- Cinnamon – 1 teaspoon
- Ground cloves – ¼ teaspoon
- Vanilla extract – 1 teaspoon
- Ground ginger – ¼ teaspoon
- Ground ginger – ¼ teaspoon
- Ground allspice – ¼ teaspoon
- Water – 1 cup

Instructions

1. Grease casserole dish that fits in the instant pot using butter then set aside
2. Add all of the crust ingredients into a mixing bowl then mix well. Place the mixture into a springform pan then press down and freeze for about 15 minutes.

3. In a mixing bowl add all of the ingredients apart from water then blend until well combined.

4. Remove springform from the freezer then pour the pumpkin pie filling into it. Use a spatula to evenly distribute the mixture.

5. Place trivet inside the instant pot then add water and place the springform gently inside. Cover with the casserole dish than as well cover the instant pot and set the valve to sealed.

6. Set time manually to 35 minutes then release pressure naturally for about 15 minutes then open the lid.

7. Remove from the instant pot then allow the pumpkin to cool and refrigerate for about 4 hours.

8. Serve with some homemade vanilla or some cinnamon ice cream

Instant Pot Apple Crisp

The uniqueness of this recipe lies in the fact that you can alternate the various types of apples that you can use. It is such a delicious dessert and can be made with the available fresh apples.

Prep Time:	10 minutes	Calories:	371
Cook Time:	18 minutes	Fat (g):	19
Total Time:	28 minutes	Protein (g):	2
Servings:	8	Net carbs (g):	64

Ingredients:

- Apples – peeled, cored and also sliced
- Granulated sugar – ¼ cup
- Lemon juice – 1 teaspoon
- Packed brown sugar – 1/3 cup
- All-purpose flour – 1/3 cup
- Rolled oats – 1/3 cup
- Melted butter – 2 tablespoons
- Cinnamon – ½ teaspoon
- Pinch of salt

Instructions:

1. Add a cup of water into the instant pot then place the trivet inside as well.
2. Grease push pan with cooking spray aside.
3. In a bowl, toss together granulated sugar, sliced apple, cinnamon and lemon juice.
4. Pour the sugared apples into the greased pan then in the same bowl, mix together rolled oats, brown sugar and salt.
5. Pour oat mixture over the apples then create a foil sling then use it to cover the push pan together with a paper towel.
6. Lower it into the instant pot then close the lid and set the valve to sealing.
7. Cook on high pressure for about 8 minutes then quick-release pressure.
8. Remove from the pot once ready then allow to cool and serve.

Butterscotch Bundt Cake

This is such a delicious cake with an appealing denser texture. Bundt cakes are lighter and also fluffier if cooked using instant pot. The cake is moist and one can alternate the ingredients as desired.

Prep Time:	13 minutes	Calories:	350
Cook Time:	35 minutes	Fat (g):	15
Total Time:	48 minutes	Protein (g):	6
Servings:	10	Net carbs (g):	47

Ingredients:

- Melted butter – 1/4cup
- Yellowcake mix – 1 box
- Pumpkin puree – 1cup
- Eggs – 5
- Vanilla extract – 1 teaspoon
- Whole milk – ¼ cup
- Butterscotch pudding mix – 1 3.4 ounce
- Pumpkin pie spice – 2 teaspoons
- Baking powder – 1.5 teaspoon
- Chopped whole pecans – ½ cup
- Sea salt – ¼ teaspoon

Instructions:

1. Place butter into a cup then microwaves for about 20 seconds.
2. In a food processor add cake mix, melted butter, pudding mix, eggs, milk, pumpkin puree, pumpkin pie spice, salt and vanilla extract then process for about 2 minutes until smooth.
3. Add the chopped pecans then pulse for a second. Grease the cake pan using butter then pour in the mixture.
4. Add one and a half cup of water into the instant pot then place into the pot the trivet. Place cake pan over the trivet then lock the lid and set to cook over high pressure for about 35 minutes.
5. Release pressure naturally for about 10 minutes then remove once cooked and allow to cool for about 10 minutes.

6. Serve the cake with some butterscotch whipped cream

Instant Pot Flan

This traditional recipe is quite rich, creamy and also very silky smooth. The caramel topping added to it is also worth the effort as it's very delicious.

Prep Time:	15 minutes	Calories:	229
Cook Time:	14 minutes	Fat (g):	5
Total Time:	29 minutes	Protein (g):	6
Servings:	8	Net carbs (g):	28

Ingredients:

- Evaporated milk – ½ can
- Sweetened condensed milk – ½ can
- Eggs – 3
- Cream cheese – 4 oz
- Granulated sugar – ½ cup
- Water – 2 cups

Instructions:

1. Place a skillet over medium heat then add sugar and heat as you occasionally stir.
2. Pour the caramel into a flan pan and ensure it spreads evenly at the bottom of the pan.
3. Coat flan mold then set it aside. Add all of the ingredients apart from water into a blender then blend until well mixed.
4. Add the mixture into flan pan then cover the flan pan.
5. Add 3 cups of water into the instant pot then insert trivet and set the flan pan over the trivet.
6. Cook it on high pressure for about 14 minutes. Once the time is up, release pressure naturally then set on an open space to cool for about 10 minutes.
7. Once cool refrigerate it for about 3 hours then unmold and serve.

Brownies with Pumpkin

These instant pot brownies are full of flavor, moist and also fudgy. You can increase the spices as per your taste. You can also alternate the ingredients with those that appeal to you. You can consider using chopped walnuts instead of the almonds.

Prep Time:	5 minutes	Calories:	242
Cook Time:	20 minutes	Fat (g):	12
Total Time:	25 minutes	Protein (g):	2
Servings:	6	Net carbs (g):	32

Ingredients:

- Oil – 1/3 cup
- Pumpkin puree – 1/3 cup
- Apple sauce – 2 tablespoons
- Vanilla extract – 1 teaspoon
- Granulated sugar – ½ cup
- Unsweetened cocoa powder -3 tablespoons
- Almond milk – 1/3 cup
- Plain flour – ¾ cup
- Almond flakes – 3 tablespoons
- Baking powder – 1 teaspoon
- Pumpkin pie spice – 1teaspoon
- Pinch of salt
- Water – 1 ½ cup

Instructions:

1. Lightly oil cake tin then set aside.
2. In a bowl mix together pumpkin puree, oil, apple sauce, almond milk, sugar and vanilla extract into a bowl until well combined.
3. Add the remaining ingredients apart from water ten mix well until combined. Pour brownie batter into the cake tin then place a trivet inside the instant pot.
4. Cover the cake tin with foil then place over the trivet. Cover the lid of the instant pot then set vent to sealing. Select manual pressure then cooks on high pressure for about 20 minutes.

5. Release pressure naturally when done for about 15 minutes then remove brownie from the pot and place on a rack.
6. Allow to cool completely then serve.

Banana Pudding Cheesecake

This is a very tasty and delicious cheesecake that's also easy to make. You can make alternate the ingredients as desired and even add lemon or orange as desired. You can top it up with some homemade whipped cream, cookie crumbs or even bananas as desired.

Prep Time:	10 minutes	Calories:	239
Cook Time:	40 minutes	Fat (g):	9
Total Time:	50 minutes	Protein (g):	7
Servings:	6	Net carbs (g):	32

Ingredients:

For crust:

- Whole pecans – ½ cup chopped
- Melted butter – 2 teaspoon
- Vanilla wafers – 14

Filling:

- Cream cheese – 16 oz
- White sugar – ½ cup
- All-purpose flour – 2 teaspoons
- Egg yolk – 1 egg
- Heavy whipping cream – ¼ cup
- Light brown sugar – 2 tablespoons
- Lemon juice – 1 teaspoon
- Large banana – 3
- Vanilla extract – ½ teaspoon
- Vanilla wafers – 20
- Eggs – 2

Topping:

- Sour cream – ½ cup
- White sugar – 1 tablespoon
- Homemade whipped cream for garnish – ½ cup

Instructions:

1. To prepare crust, add pecans into a food processor then pulse until formed into crumbs.

2. Add melted butter then pulse again for a few seconds until well combined.

3. Pour the mixture at the bottom of cheesecake pan that's greased then press the mixture well at the bottom.

4. Line the pan with the 14 mini cookies then place into the freezer and allow to stay for about 15 minutes.

5. To prepare the filling, mash a banana using a fork into a bowl then add lemon juice, and brown sugar to bowl and mix until the sugar is well dissolved.

6. Chop the remaining bananas then add to the bowl and mix well then set aside.

7. Pour the mixture into a food processor then blend together with the cream cheese, heavy cream, sugar, vanilla extract and flour until smooth.

8. Add ten mini cookies into the mixture then combine.

9. Pour the filling into the greased cheesecake pan then use a spatula to push cookies into the filing until evenly distributed.

10. To bake the cake, add one an half cups of water to the bottom of the instant pot then place the trivet inside.

11. Place cheesecake into the pot then covers the pot using a paper towel and aluminum foil. Lock the lid and set valve to sealing.

12. Cook it on high pressure for about 40 minutes then naturally release pressure for 15 minutes.

Instant Pot Peach Crisp

This is a perfect summertime dessert that's prepared with fresh and juicy peaches and can be topped with some crunchy oatmeal for a fulfilling taste. You can serve it with some vanilla ice cream or whatever you prefer.

Prep Time:	5 minutes	Calories:	299
Cook Time:	25 minutes	Fat (g):	8
Total Time:	30 minutes	Protein (g):	6
Servings:	8	Net carbs (g):	53

Ingredients:

Peach crisp topping:

- Butter- ½ cup
- Oats – 1 ½ cups
- All-purpose flour – ½ cup
- Brown sugar – ¾ cup
- Chopped pecans – ½ cup
- Salt – ½ teaspoon

Peach filling

- Peach wedges – 8 cups (7 ripe peaches)
- Granulated sugar – ¼ cup
- Brown sugar – ¼ cup
- Vanilla extract – 1 teaspoon
- Cornstarch – 2 tablespoon
- Lemon juice – 1 teaspoon
- Water – 2 tablespoon
- Cinnamon powder – ½ teaspoon

Instructions:

1. For the peach crisp topping, in a bowl combine flour, oats, pecans, salt and sugar then mix together.
2. Melt butter in a frying pan over medium heat then add the mixture into the pan.

3. Stir it frequently for about 8 minutes then pour the mixture into a parchment paper and allow to cool.
4. To prepare peach filling, add all of the filling ingredients apart from water into a bowl then stir to combine.
5. Pour the mixture inside the instant pot then close the pot and allow to cook for 4 minutes over high pressure.
6. Release pressure naturally for about 10 minutes then add 2 tablespoons of water and cornstarch into the mixture and combine well.
7. Press sauté then stir in cornstarch and mix well.
8. Continue stirring for about 2 minutes or until it thickens.
9. Press cancel when ready then serve warm, in bowls as you top with the crisped topping.

Instant Pot Monkey Bread

Such a classic sweet bread that is also easy to prepare. Use of brown butter brings out that nutty taste which is quite delicious. You can alternate the ingredients as desired for that desired taste.

Prep Time:	5 minutes	Calories:	176
Cook Time:	25 minutes	Fat (g):	8
Total Time:	30 minutes	Protein (g):	1
Servings:	8	Net carbs (g):	27

Ingredients:

- Non-stick spray for the baking pan
- Unsalted butter – 3 tablespoons
- Ground cinnamon – 1 tablespoon
- Refrigerated biscuits – 1 (16.3 ounces)
- Confectioner's sugar – ½ cup
- Turbinado sugar – ½ cup

Instructions:

1. Light spray the baking pan using cooking spray then set aside
2. Turn instant pot to sauté then allow to heat for about 5 minutes.
3. Add butter and cook for about 3 minutes then turn the heat off. Pour batter into a bowl then add a cup of water into the instant pot.
4. Instant rack into the pot then combine sugar in a bowl, and cinnamon then mixes together and sprinkle the mixture at the bottom of the baking pan.
5. Roll biscuit pieces in the melted brown butter and cinnamon and sugar mixture then arrange at the bottom of the pan.
6. Cover the top of the pan with foil then carefully lower into the instant pan. Cover the instant pot then cook for about 25 minutes on high pressure.
7. In a different bowl, combine confectioner's sugar and a teaspoon of water into a bowl then whisk together.
8. Once the bread is ready, release pressure naturally then allows to cool.
9. Drizzle the monkey bread with the glaze then serve immediately.

Bread Pudding

This is a classic brunch staple that's very delicious. You can add that crispy crust by placing the dish under the broiler for a few minutes after preparing it.

Prep Time:	10 minutes	Calories:	425
Cook Time:	1 hour	Fat (g):	19
Total Time:	1 hour 10 minutes	Protein (g):	14
Servings:	8	Net carbs (g):	47

Ingredients:

- Unsalted butter – 1 tablespoon
- Cubed challah – 8 cups
- Milk – 2 cups
- Heavy cream – 3 cups
- Vanilla extract – 1 tablespoon
- Fine salt – ½ teaspoon
- Ground cinnamon – ¼ teaspoon
- Egg yolks – 6
- Raisins- ½ cup optional
- Sugar – 1 ¼ cups

Instructions:

1. Grease the baking dish with melted butter then set aside.
2. Add bread cubes into the baking dish then bake in the oven a 300^0F for about 20 minutes or until dry.
3. In a bowl, add milk, cream, eggs and the egg yolks, cinnamon, salt, vanilla and sugar then whisk together. Add bread and the raisins then stir until well coated.
4. Pour the mixture into the greased baking dish then cover the dish with foil.
5. Add 2 cups of water into the instant pot then insert the rack. Lower the baking dish into the pot the lock the lid of the instant pot and cook on high pressure for about 45 minutes.
6. Quick-release pressure then removes from the pot and allow to cool.
7. Serve at the desired temperature.

Instant Pot Orange Cake

This is such a delicious orange cake that can be topped with orange syrup for enhanced flavor. It is easy to make, fluffy and very moist cake that has an amazing orange flavor.

Prep Time:	10 minutes	Calories:	270
Cook Time:	30 minutes	Fat (g):	8
Total Time:	40 minutes	Protein (g):	4
Servings:	8	Net carbs (g):	45

Ingredients:

- Peeled Orange – 1 large
- All-purpose flour – 1 ½ cups
- White sugar – 1 cup
- Vegetable oil – ½ cup
- Baking soda – 1 ½ teaspoon
- Salt – ¼ teaspoon

Instructions:

1. Get the baking pan greased
2. Blend orange using a blender until liquefied then measure one cup of orange juice.
3. Whisk the orange juice, vegetable oil, sugar, baking soda and salt together into a large bowl then pour the mixture into the greased pan.
4. Add a cup of water into the instant pot then add the trivet. Cover the cooking pan with foil then place over the trivet inside the pot.
5. Let it cook on high pressure for 30 minutes then release pressure naturally for 10 minutes
6. Remove from the instant pot once ready then allow toll.
7. Serve at the desired temperature.

Instant Pot Carrot Cake Oatmeal

Such a filling and nutritious instant pot carrot cake oatmeal. It's not only nutritious but also quite easy to prepare. You can also alternate the ingredients as desired.

Prep Time:	15 minutes	Calories:	351
Cook Time:	10 minutes	Fat (g):	13
Total Time:	25 minutes	Protein (g):	10
Servings:	4	Net carbs (g):	48

Ingredients:

- Lemon Juice, fresh -1/4 teaspoon
- Carrot, grated -1 cup
- Vanilla Extract -1 teaspoon
- Cinnamon, grounded-1 teaspoon
- Almond Milk, unsweetened -11/4 cup
- Rolled Oats -1/2 cup
- Maple Syrup -1 tablespoon +1 teaspoon
- Ginger, grounded-1/4teaspoon
- Pinch of Salt
- Dash of Nutmeg, grounded

Instructions:

1. Mix almond milk, nutmeg, maple syrup, salt, cinnamon, and ginger in a medium pot until well combined.
2. Add a cup of water into the instant pot then press on porridge and cook the mixture for five minutes.
3. Stir in the carrot and oats then stir and cook on high pressure with the lid covered for about 10 minutes. Release pressure naturally once has done then allow to cool
4. Spoon in the vanilla extract then stir again and transfer it to the serving bowl
5. Top it with your choice of topping.

Pumpkin Casserole

Prep Time:	15 minutes	Calories:	169
Cook Time:	25 minutes	Fat (g):	14
Total Time:	40 minutes	Protein (g):	9
Servings:	8	Net carbs (g):	13

Ingredients:

- Pumpkin - 200 g
- Curd - 500 g
- Semolina - 3 tablespoons
- Chicken eggs - 2
- Buttermilk - 100 ml

- Baking powder - 1 teaspoon
- Sugar - 2 tablespoons
- Ground cinnamon - to taste
- Butter - 1 teaspoon

Instructions:

1. Put cottage cheese, eggs, buttermilk, baking powder and sugar in one dish. Beat with a mixer until smooth. No mixer - use a whisk or a fork. Do not like grains of cottage cheese - pass it through a sieve, and then mix with the rest of the ingredients.
2. In a blender bowl, mashed boiled pumpkin with honey, semolina and cinnamon (this ingredient is optional). No blender - use a meat grinder or just crush pumpkin with a fork.
3. Grease the instant pot bowl with butter, put the curd and pumpkin mass in the center of the bottom of the bowl in portions, one at a time (two tablespoons of one, two tablespoons of the other, and so on to the end). Select manual pressure then cooks on high pressure for about 25 minutes.
4. Release pressure naturally then let it cool for 10 minutes.

Jam Pie

Prep Time:	15 minutes	Calories:	399
Cook Time:	40 minutes	Fat (g):	8
Total Time:	55 minutes	Protein (g):	15
Servings:	8	Net carbs (g):	61

Ingredients:

- Margarine - 120 g
- Eggs - 2
- Sugar - 150 g
- Wheat flour - 350 g
- Baking soda - 0.5 teaspoon
- Jam - 150 g

Instructions:

1. It is better to take a thick jam, but if you have a liquid, do not worry, add a couple of teaspoons of starch. If you use only yolks instead of eggs, then the dough will be softer. In this case, reduce the flour by 50-60 grams.

2. First, beat the eggs with sugar.

3. Add margarine to the egg-sugar mixture. Mix it well. Chop margarine with a knife into small crumbs.

4. Add soda and mix.

5. Add the sifted flour. Knead the dough.

6. Chop the dough with a knife. Then add flour and chop. You get such a dense lumpy mass.

7. Then knead the dough with your hands, form a bun, wrap it in a bag and put it in the refrigerator for 30 minutes.

8. After half an hour take out the dough, divide it into two unequal parts. About 3/4 and 1/4, line the bowl with two strips of parchment to make the cake easier to get out. Roll the dough into a circle slightly larger than the diameter of the instant pot bowl, put it in the bowl, and form small sides.

9. Spread the jam not to the edge of the sides.

10. Sprinkle slices (balls) of the remaining dough on top of the jam. Select manual pressure then cooks on high pressure for about 40 minutes. Release pressure naturally then let it cool for 10 minutes.

11. Enjoy your meal.

Currant Pie

Prep Time:	15 minutes	Calories:	257
Cook Time:	20 minutes	Fat (g):	11
Total Time:	35 minutes	Protein (g):	4
Servings:	8	Net carbs (g):	39

Ingredients:

- Butter - 100 g
- Sugar - 200 g
- Flour - 200 g
- Milk - 250 ml
- Baking powder - 2 tsp

- Eggs - 3
- Vanilla sugar
- Currants (assorted) - 250 g

Instructions:

1. Beat soft butter with sugar.
2. Add eggs and warm milk. Mix.
3. Add flour sifted with baking powder and mix.
4. Sprinkle currants with two tablespoons of flour. Berries can also be taken frozen, in which case they do not need to be thawed, just sprinkle with flour.
5. Pour currants into the dough and mix gently, being careful not to mash the berries.
6. Grease the instant pot bowl with butter and pour the dough into it.
7. Select manual pressure then cooks on high pressure for about 20 minutes. Release pressure naturally then let it cool for 10 minutes.
8. Sprinkle with powdered sugar. Enjoy your meal!

Conclusion

Baking has always been and will continue to be a passionate affair. However, the world is changing, and aesthetics tend to drive towards maximization of space as much as possible. This means less bulky appliances, eradication of strenuous techniques and generally, giving a less crowded décor.

To the ardent baker, this might translate into elimination of large ovens, stoves, pots, pans, and other bulky kitchen wares. In its place then comes the new school; the instant pot and the likes. However, your baking life does not have to suffer as you can achieve a reasonable amount of baking with your instant pot.

This book has tried to make this process even more comfortable. It eliminates the stress of having to convert your recipe for instant pot use and the guesswork involved in adjusting the time to get the best results possible. It is filled with a lot of mouth-watering recipes for your baking pleasure, all measured out and timed just for you.

Simply plug in your instant pot, pick the recipe of your choice, then go ahead to make use of the new magic appliance in your kitchen. You will find out that with time, you will be able to tweak recipes and create your unique taste as your mastery of the instant pot improves.

Made in the USA
Monee, IL
18 March 2020